UNSEEN
RAIN

UNSEEN RAIN

Quatrains of

RUMI

by John Moyne and Coleman Barks

THRESHOLD BOOKS

Threshold Books is committed to publishing books of spiritual significance and high literary quality. All Threshold books have sewn bindings and are printed on acid-free paper.

We will be happy to send you a catalog.
Threshold Books, RD 4, Box 600, Putney, Vermont 05346

Library of Congress Catalog Card Number 86-050782
ISBN 0-939660-16-4

Cover illustration: an early portrait of Mevlana Jelaluddin Rumi

Introduction

In the mountains along a creek half-frozen with thick ledges of ice, a friend once handed me an icy drop of dew. I held it close to my eye like a lens. The hemlock and the rhododendron and the creek were suddenly upsidedown above me! The world reversed in a tear.

Rumi's short poems, the quatrains *(Rubaiyat)* have many tones and effects: Some of them quick, joyful whimsies— songs a carload of friends might spin off on a trip.

> Tonight, a singing competition:
> Jupiter, the moon, and myself,
> the friends I've been looking for!

Some are finely faceted, abstract statements.

> Being is not what it seems,
> nor non-being. The world's
> existence is not
> in the world.

But most do what the dewdrop did, put vast space where you thought you were standing. Like grief, they flip normal, rational perspective to sudden mystery and clarity. And like short poems from other lineages, they require a lot of emptiness, room to wander, sky, the inward space of patience and longing. They are small doors that somehow *are* the region they open into.

> I have lived on the lip
> of insanity, wanting to know reasons,
> knocking on a door. It opens.
> I've been knocking from the inside!

Rumi lived most of his life in Konya, Turkey, which in the 13th Century was a meeting-point for many cultures at the western end of the Silk Road, a connective node for Christian, Islamic, Hindu, and even Buddhist, worlds. Rumi weaves elements from these traditions into a whole, a single energy, of which these short bursts are spontaneous fragments.

Though there are suites of poems around a single image or idea, the sequence was not meant to be thematically coherent. Rumi's *Rubaiyat* is improvised music. Structural arrangement is not primary. Rumi's ideas on Friendship grow, circulate, and clarify as they take on, and explore, various images. The sequence, in fact, is not Rumi's, but his editor's, and this selection is only a small fraction of the quatrains in the *Divan*. (See the Note on the Translations.)

Here is how one of them sounds in Persian.

> *joz   eshq naebud   hich daemsaz   maera*
> except love not was any companion me-for
> *nay avvail-o   nay achaer-o   aghaz   maera*
> not first-and not last-and beginning me-for
> *jan   midaehaed aez dorunae avaz   maera*
> soul/life gives from inside call me-for
> *kay   kahel-e   rah-e eshq   daerbaz   maera*
> oh-that ignorant-of way-of love door-open me-for

The poems are sonically very dense. Clusters of similar, or identical, sounds pile quickly one upon the other. These sound patterns are very tricky to duplicate in English. So many rhyming syllables in English usually produce a trivial, light comic effect, or gibberish. We have tried to connect these poems with a strong American line of free-verse spiritual poetry. Whitman, Roethke, Snyder, James Wright. The late Cambridge Islamicist, A.J.Arberry, himself a pioneer Rumi translator, once called for such free-verse poetic translations.

Rumi's Life (1207-1273)

Born in Balkh, in what is now Afghanistan, Jelaluddin Rumi was exiled early in life by the Mongol invasions, to Konya. Following his father, he became the center of a medrese, a learning community. Konya in the mid-13th Century was, at the very least, a trilingual city. Turkish the vernacular, Persian the literary language, and Arabic the language of the Koran and religious ceremony. Rumi wrote, or more often dictated, predominantly in Persian.

Rumi's way of teaching in the medrese seems to have evolved in definite stages: From pre-Shams discourses, to the ecstatic spontaneity of the middle of his life—the strong heart-center poetry—to the later, complex combination of stories and lyricism and teachings, the *Mathnawi*, which occupied the last twelve years of his life.

The poems in this volume come from the middle period, the *Divan-i Shamsi Tabriz* (1570 pages, 42,000 lines of poetry). Rumi was thirty-seven when he met Shams in 1244, Shams about sixty. Up until then Rumi had been a fairly traditional mystic, one of a long line of scholars and theologians. Shams literally took Rumi's books, his intellectual brilliance, and threw them into a well to show him how he needed to live what he'd been reading.

The two of them went into week-long periods of *sohbet*, mystical conversation and merging. Certain people became jealous of this consuming absorption in the Friend. They drove Shams off for a time, to Damascus. But he returned, and finally, apparently, they murdered him. The legend varies. What is clear is that the deep friendship with Shams could not be tolerated. There was some danger perceived by the religious community in the continuous ecstacy of Lover and Beloved. They were separated.

The excitement of these poems, though, is that in them we overhear those two, Rumi and Shams, still in collusion. These poems are the whispering of two lovers in a crowd.

Before the contact with Shams, and the bewildering wrenching away, Rumi was not really a poet. The poetry sprang into being in celebration of the meeting with Shams and in grief and longing for the Friend's return. The poetry, also, can be seen as a unique record of the union of lover and beloved, soul and spirit, if such intensity can be called a "record." Certainly it's not linear, or completed, or explainable. He hears camel bells in the distance. When the approaching presence calls out, he says, the first word spoken will coincide exactly with the last word of his last poem. For Rumi, poetry is what he does in the meantime, a song-and-dance until the greater reality he loves arrives: A melting tear-gift eye-piece to look through, while it and the scene and the eye dissolve.

Coleman Barks
John Moyne
Jan. 30, 1986

A Note on These Translations

These are collaborative translations done by John Moyne, Head of Linguistics at the Graduate School of the City University of New York, and Coleman Barks, a poet and Associate Professor of English at the University of Georgia in Athens.

In the standard edition of Rumi's work (Badi-uz-Zaman Furuzanfar, editor, *Kulliyat-e Shams*, 8 vols., Teheran: Amir Kabir Press, 1957-66) the quatrains are numbered. We have not included these numbers in the text; however, for reference, they are:

1:3,1	29:567,569	57:1091,1092
2:2,7	30:570,573	58:1095,1109
3:20,27	31:587,670	59:1110,1111
4:29,31	32:681,682	60:1118,1119
5:32,33	33:683,684	61:1120,1122
6:42,44	34:685,720	62:1124,1125
7:51,55	35:723,724	63:1128,1129
8:57,61	36:725,728	64:1130,1133
9:62,63	37:730,731	65:1135,1138
10:67,79	38:744,745	66:1141,1148
11:86,88	39:748,751	67:1149,1150
12:93,94	40:798,800	68:1151,1152
13:97,152	41:801,804	69:1155,1159
14:153,159	42:806,807	70:1160,1164
15:163,165	43:808,809	71:1169,1184
16:166,167	44:814,822	72:1185,1194
17:168,169	45:823,825	73:1196,1228
18:170,171	46:827,828	74:1233,1240
19:173,181	47:830,831	75:1247,1249
20:317,318	48:837,841	76:1296,1299
21:319,321	49:904,907	77:1301,1305
22:322,326	50:910,911	78:1306,1307
23:329,330	51:912,915	79:1311,1320
24:331,333	52:917,925	80:1798,1854
25:334,337	53:926,927	81:1642,1645
26:338,394	54:1022,1035	82:1653,1784
27:401,491	55:1080,1083	83:1325,1352
28:546,561	56:1084,1086	

Dedicated to Bawa Muhaiyaddeen

The one who floods the private sanctuary
I've built, who takes away sleep,
who drags and throws me under,
that presence is the joy I speak.

The center clears. Knowing comes:
The body is not singular like a corpse,
but singular like a salt grain
still in the side of the mountain.

The light you give off
did not come from a pelvis.
Your features did not begin in semen.
Don't try to hide inside anger
radiance that cannot be hidden.

All day and night, music,
a quiet, bright
reedsong. If it
fades, we fade.

Sleep this year has no authority.
Night might as well stop looking for us
when we're like this,
invisible, except at dawn.

This night extends into eternity,
like a fire burning inside the Friend.
Truly knowing this is what joy is.
Forgetting it is grief, and a lack of courage.

Days are sieves to filter spirit,
reveal impurities, and too,
show the light of some who throw
their own shining into the universe.

Out of nowhere a horse
brought us here where we taste love
until we don't exist again. This taste
is the wine we always mention.

Earlier, to be ready,
I loosened the leg bindings.
Today, your scent. Gratefulness
rises on the air.

These gifts from the Friend, a robe
of skin and veins, a teacher within,
wear them and become a school,
with a greater Sheikh nearby.

There is no companion but love.
No starting, or finishing, yet, a road.
The Friend calls from there:
Why do you hesitate when lives are in danger!

I pretended to leap
to see if I could live *there.*

Someday I must actually arrive *there,*
or nothing will be left to arrive.

Here's a magnificent person
holding out a glass of wine,
a vision of power.
Over me, I hope, not *for* me!

Let the lover be disgraceful, crazy,
absentminded. Someone sober
will worry about events going badly.
Let the lover be.

The manner and appearance of a prophet,
our secret origins, these are born
of a woman who still lives inside us,
though she's hiding from what we've become.

If you have a spirit, lose it,
loose it to return where with one word,
we came from. Now, thousands of words,
and we refuse to leave.

If you want to live, leave your banks,
as a small stream enters the Oxus, miles wide,
or as cattle moving around a millstone
suddenly circle to the top of the sphere.

Life is ending? God gives another.
Admit the finite. Praise the infinite.
Love is a spring. Submerge.
Every separate drop, a new life.

I thought I had self-control,
so I regretted times I didn't.

With that considering over, the one thing I know
is I don't know who I am.

This piece of food cannot be eaten,
nor this bit of wisdom found by looking.
There is a secret core in everyone
not even Gabriel can know by trying to know.

You come to reading books late in life.
Don't worry if you see the young ones
ahead of you. Don't hurry.
You're tired and ready to quit?
Let your hands play music.

Some nights, stay up till dawn,
as the moon sometimes does for the sun.
Be a full bucket pulled up the dark way
of a well, then lifted out into light.

Tonight remove whatever remains.

Last night we lay listening to your one story,
of being in love. We lay around you,
stunned like the dead.

No wineglasses here, but wine is handed round.
No smoke, but burning.

Listen to the unstruck sounds,
and what sifts through that music.

We don't need wine to get drunk,
or instruments and singing to feel ecstatic.
No poets, no leaders, no songs,
yet we jump around totally wild.

No better love than love with no object,
no more satsifying work than work with no purpose.

If you could give up tricks and cleverness,
that would be the cleverest trick!

I can break off from anyone,
except that presence within.

Anyone can bring gifts.
Give me someone who takes away.

Noah's ark is the symbol of our species,
a boat wandering the ocean.

A plant grows deep in the center of that water.
It has no form and no location.

What is this day with two suns in the sky?
Day unlike other days,
with a great voice giving it to the planet,
Here it is, enamored beings, your day!

Glass of wine in hand, I fall,
get on my feet again, dizzy, deranged,
then sink down demolished,
not in this place any longer,
yet here, strong and sober, still standing.

The Friend comes clapping, at once obvious
and obscure, without fear or plans.

I am like I am
because this one is like that.

The Friend comes into my body
looking for the center, unable
to find it, draws a blade,
strikes anywhere.

This night there are no limits to what may be given.
This is not a night but a marriage,
a couple whispering in bed in unison the same words.
Darkness simply lets down a curtain for that.

Tonight is the essence of night,
asking and what the asking wants,
generosity and the given,
something said back and forth,
with God!

A night full of talking that hurts,
my worst held-back secrets: Everything
has to do with loving and not loving.
This night will pass.
Then we have work to do.

I circle your nest tonight,
around and around until morning
when a breath of air says, *Now,*
and the Friend holds up like a goblet
some anonymous skull.

I am filled with you.
Skin, blood, bone, brain, and soul.
There's no room for lack of trust, or trust.
Nothing in this existence but that existence.

Don't forget the nut, being so proud of the shell,
The body has its inward ways,

the five senses. They crack open,
and the Friend is revealed.

Crack open the Friend, you become
the All-One.

Keep walking, though there's no place to get to.
Don't try to see through the distances.
That's not for human beings. Move within,
but don't move the way fear makes you move.

Walk to the well.
Turn as the earth and the moon turn,
circling what they love.
Whatever circles comes from the center.

The rose laughs at my long-looking,
my constantly wondering what
a *rose* means, and who *owns*
the rose, whatever it means.

Two hands, two feet, two eyes, good,
as it should be, but no separation
of the Friend and your loving.

Any dividing there
makes other untrue distinctions like "Jew,"
and "Christian," and "Muslim."

Seeing you heals me.
Not seeing you, I feel the walls closing.
I would not wish for anyone else
such absence.

What keeps you alive without me?
How can you cry?
How can you know who you are?
How can you see?

Lost to one who seems not care,
I feel pain, though even that is welcome
from the Other who demands everything I am.

If I withhold it for now,
as worthless, the asking is precious.

My love hides on the path where the love-thief goes
and catches that one by the hair with my teeth.
Who are you? the love-thief asks, but as I open
my mouth to say, he escapes into the desert.

I thought of you and threw
my glass of wine against the wall.

Now I'm neither drunk nor sober,
jumping up and down, completely mad.

Our eyes do not see you,
but we have this excuse: Eyes
see surface, not reality,
though we keep hoping,
in this lovely place.

After being with me one whole night,
you ask how I live when you're not here.

Badly, frantically, like a fish trying to breathe
dry sand. You weep and say,
But you choose that.

There is a channel between voice and presence,
a way where information flows.

In disciplined silence the channel opens.
With wandering talk, it closes.

Day ferments. Eyes moisten with clouds.
Wind shakes trees, and they laugh,
just as the playful racket of children
happens, because mothers cry out
and fathers reach to touch.

You have said what you are.
I am what I am.
Your actions in my head,
my head here in my hands
with something circling inside.
I have no name
for what circles
so perfectly.

Why all this grief and turning pale?
Don't look at me.
Like any face reflecting other light,
the moon is a source of pain.

Someone who sees you and does not laugh out loud,
or fall silent, or explode in pieces,
is nothing more than the cement
and stone of his own prison.

Step barefooted on the ground and make it giddy,
pregnant with joking and buds.
A Spring uproar rises into the stars.
The moon begins to wonder what's going on.

Those of you in the nightsky above the moon,
try walking damp ground.
Ecstatic singers in sacred taverns,
get up at dawn. Try not sleeping.

A secret turning in us
makes the universe turn.
Head unaware of feet,
and feet head. Neither cares.
They keep turning.

This moment this love comes to rest in me,
many beings in one being.
In one wheat-grain a thousand sheaf stacks.
Inside the needle's eye, a turning night of stars.

Courage: A gazelle turns
to face a pack of lions.
A building that stands on bedrock, stands.
Do you think my love will slump to the ground
when you leave?

Again, I'm within my self.
I walked away, but here I come sailing back,
feet in the air, upsidedown,
as a saint when he opens his eyes
from prayer: Now. The room,
the tablecloth, familiar faces.

Listen, if you can stand to.
Union with the Friend means not being who you've been,
being instead silence: A place: A view
where language is inside seeing.

Don't think of good advice for me.
I've tasted the worst that can happen.
So they lock me somewhere, bound and gagged,
they can't tie up this new love I have.

In the shambles of love, they kill only the best,
none of the weak or deformed.
Don't run away from this dying.
Whoever's not killed for love is carrion.

Being is not what it seems,
nor non-being. The world's
existence is not
in the world.

When your love reaches the core,
earth-heavals and bright irruptions spew in the air.

The universe becomes one spiritual thing, that simple,
love mixing with spirit.

Who ever saw such drunkards?
Barrels broken open, the ground and starry
ceiling soaked. And look,
this full glass in my hand.

No intellect denies that you are,
but no one gives in completely to that.

This is not a place where you are not,
yet not a place where you are seen.

One day you will take me completely out of my self,
I'll do what the angels cannot do.

Your eyelash will write on my cheek
the poem that hasn't been thought of.

Inside water, a waterwheel turns.
A star circulates with the moon.

We live in the night ocean wondering,
What are these lights?

From the wet source someone
cuts a reed to make a flute.
The reed sips breath like wine,
sips more, practicing. Now drunk,
it starts the high clear notes.

At first, I sang and recited poems,
keeping the neighbors awake.
Now more intense, quieter.
When the fire flames up, smoke vanishes.

When you confine, I'm free.
If you rebuke, I'm honored.

Your dividing blade is love.
Your moaning, song.

Listen to presences inside poems.
Let them take you where they will.

Follow those private hints,
and never leave the premises.

Drunks fear the police,
but the police are drunk too.

People in this town love them both
like different chess pieces.

Night goes back to where it was.
Everyone returns home sometime.

Night, when you get there,
tell them how I love you.

Night comes so people can sleep like fish
in black water. Then day.

Some people pick up their tools.
Others become the making itself.

A voice inside both of us sings out
a few lines from Khusraw, a stanza from Shirin.

At times a calm voice excites us.
Other times excited words make us quiet.

The morning wind spreads its fresh smell.
We must get up and take that in,
that wind that lets us live.
Breathe, before it's gone.

I am so small I can barely be seen.
How can this great love be inside me?

Look at your eyes. They are small,
but they see enormous things.

Where is a foot worthy to walk a garden,
or an eye that deserves to look at trees?

Show me a man willing to be
thrown in the fire.

You speak and I start laughing.
Corpses come to life.
I'm trying not to talk gibberish today,
though totally lost and wandering.

No one is ever depressed with you.
Those receiving light give out light.

Secrets cannot be kept
from a confidante.

Who says the eternal being does not exist?
Who says the sun has gone out?

Someone who climbs up on the roof, and closes his eyes tight,
and says, *I don't see anything.*

When you feel your lips becoming infinite
and sweet, like the moon in a sky,
when you feel that spaciousness inside,
Shams of Tabriz will be there too.

A ruby with a sweet taste,
absorbing wine-light. I could tell you
the name of this grape, but why?
I serve one who keeps secrets.

Already tightly bound, we are wrapped with yet another chain.
We've lost everything, but here's another disaster.
Held in the curls of your hair,
we feel a rope around our neck.

Those on the way are almost invisible
to those who are not. A man or a woman
recognizes God and starts out. The others
say he, or she, is losing faith.

I want a poet who cannot leave the Friend.
If he could, and still be always in love,
he would be a master, or he couldn't.
Give us poets like that.

The sun is love. The lover,
a speck circling the sun.

A Spring wind moves to dance
any branch that isn't dead.

Don't let your throat tighten
with fear. Take sips of breath
all day and night. Before death
closes your mouth.

If I gave up sanity,
I could fill a hundred versions of you.

There is no liquid like a tear
from a lover's eye.

I honor those who try
to rid themselves of any lying,
who empty the self
and have only clear being there.

God only knows, I don't,
what keeps me laughing.

The stem of a flower
moves when the air moves.

I reach for a piece of wood. It turns into a lute.
I do some meanness. It turns out helpful.
I say one must not travel during the holy month.
Then I start out, and wonderful things happen.

Never too many fish in a swift creek,
never too much water for fish to live in.

No place is too small for lovers,
nor can lovers see too much of the world.

An ecstatic seed planted anywhere on earth
comes up with this crop we plant.

The music of a reed flute heard anywhere
floats in the air as proof of our loving.

I say, *Bring the simple wine that makes me loose and free.*
You say, *There's a hurricane coming!*
And I say, *Let's have some wine then,*
and sit here like old statues and watch.

The prophets all were commanded
to stay in the company of lovers.

We take warmth from fire, but fire
goes out in the presence of ashes.

I planted roses, but without you they were thorns.
I hatched peacock eggs. Snakes were inside.
Played the harp, sour music.
I went to the eighth heaven. It was the lowest hell.

I say what I think I should do.
        You say *Die*
I say my lamp's oil has turned to water.
        You say *Die*.
I say I burn like a moth in the candle
        of your face. You say *Die*.

Eyes. You say *Keep them open.*
Liver. You say *Keep it working.*
I mention the heart-center. You ask *What is there?*
Much love for you. *Keep it for yourself.*

Secrets try to enter our ears. Don't prevent them.
Don't hide your face. Don't let us
be without music and wine. Don't let us
breathe once without being where you are.

We're confused as lovers always are.
You walk in and out among the confusions,
unaffected, but anyone trying to follow you
will be confused.

Every day, this pain. Either you're numb
or you don't understand love.
I write out my love story.
You see the writing, but you don't read it.

The sun coming up brings clear wine-air.
Being sober is not living.
Listen to the longing of a stringless harp.
Stand watch over this burning.

You come closer, though you never left.
Water flows, and the stream stays full.
You are a bag of musk. We are the fragrance.
Is musk ever separated from its scent?

Whispering at dawn:
"Don't keep from me what you know."

Answer: *Some things are to understand
but not say. Be quiet.*

I saw you last night in the gathering,
but could not take you openly in my arms,
so I put my lips next to your cheek,
pretending to talk privately.

I want to hold you close like a lute
so we can cry out with loving.

You would rather throw stones at a mirror?
I am your mirror, and here are the stones.

Someone who does not bloom at the sight of you
is empty and numb like a drum stored away.

Someone who does not enjoy the names of God
                and the words of prophets
remains apart from those.

Something opens our wings. Something
makes boredom and hurt disappear.
Someone fills the cup in front of us:
We taste only sacredness.

Inside wisdom, a bright-flowing, analytic power.
Inside love, a friend.
One a psychic source, the other plain water.

Walk out into the indications
of where you must go.

Christ is the population of the world,
and every object as well. There is no room
for hypocrisy. Why use bitter soup for healing
when sweet water is everywhere?

My ego is stubborn, often drunk, impolite.
My loving: Finely sensitive, impatient, confused.
Please take messages from one to the other,
reply and counter-reply.

I'll never look for somewhere else to live,
no longer shy about how I love. My eyes open.
You are everywhere: Collyrium: Medicine, for
clearing sight and strengthening circulation.

Love comes sailing through and I scream.
Love sits beside me like a private supply of itself.
Love puts away the instruments,
and takes off the silk robes. Our nakedness
together changes me completely.

Much commotion at your door,
all attention drawn that way.

Remember, even though I've done terrible things,
I can still see the whole world in your face.

The wine forbidden in this place
creates life for the inner being.
Fill with that and forget consequences.
There's no beginning or end.

I hear you and I'm everywhere, a spreading music.
You've done this many times.
You already own me, but once more
you buy me back into being.

Lightning, your presence
from ground to sky.
No one knows what becomes of me,
when you take me so quickly.

The wind is what you say.
The night bird is drunk with the syllables of your name,
over and over, like the strokes of a portrait
being carefully painted in the tall space inside of me.

Birdsong, wind,
the water's face.

Each flower, remembering the smell:
I know you're closeby.

I love this giving my life to you,
or to anyone who knows someone who knows you,
caught as I am in your curling hair,
inside your Kashmiri-witch eyes.

Held like this, to draw in milk,
no will, tasting clouds of milk,
never so content.

Since I've been away from you,
I only know how to weep.

Like a candle, melting is who I am.
Like a harp, any sound I make is music.

What I most want
is to spring out of this personality,
then to sit apart from that leaping.
I've lived too long where I can be reached.

Happy, not from anything that happens.
Warm, not from fire or a hot bath.
Light, I register zero on a scale.

Burning with longing-fire,
wanting to sleep with my head on your doorsill,
my living is composed only of this trying
to be in your presence.

Begin as creation, become a creator.
Never wait at a barrier.
In this kitchen stocked with fresh food,
why sit content with a cup of warm water?

I stand up, and this one of me
turns into a hundred of me.
They say I circle around you.
Nonsense. I circle around me.

I can't tell my secrets.
I have no key to that door.
Something keeps me joyful,
but I cannot say what.

Tonight, a singing competition:
Jupiter, the moon, and myself,
the friends I've been looking for!

Tonight with wine being poured
and instruments singing among themselves,
one thing is forbidden,
one thing: Sleep.

When longing is sharp,
and the ruby color deep,
we welcome your grief,
but don't bring ambition or wanting,
or sleepy boredom.

Full moon. Quietly awake,
you look down from a corner of the roof,
reminding us it's not time
to sleep, or to drink wine.

Tonight we're getting love-messages.
For their sake we must not go to sleep.
The fragrance of your hair spreading through the stree
makes the perfumers wonder at such competition.

Grapes under feet that crush them
turn whichever way they are turned.

You ask why I turn around you?
Not around you, I turn around myself.

Gone, inner and outer,
no moon, no ground or sky.
Don't hand me another glass of wine.
Pour it in my mouth.
I've lost the way to my mouth.

Hunted down, yet hunter.
Without a job, yet constantly working.
Do you want my head? Friend,
I make you a gift.

What is real is you and my love
for you. High in the air, unnoticed,
this reality rises into a dome.
I am the Capella!

I came and sat in front of you
as I would at an altar.
Every promise I made before
I broke when I saw you.

Don't come to us without bringing music.
We celebrate with drum and flute,
with wine not made from grapes,
in a place you cannot imagine.

Joyful for no reason,
I want to see beyond this existence.

You open your lips, laughing.
I think of a design for that opening.

As long as I can remember, I've wanted you.
I've made a monument of this loving.

I had a dream last night, but it's gone now.
All I know is I woke up like this again.

Drawn by your growing,
we gather like disheveled hair.
Even spirits come to bow,
We were dead. Now we are back.

My turban, my robe, my head, those three
for less than a penny.
My self, my name, not to be mentioned,
less than nothing.

At night you come here secretly,
and I want the darkness not to end.

But Night says, *Look, you're holding the sun.
So you're in charge of daylight!*

The secret you told, tell again.
If you refuse, I'll start crying.
Then you'll say, *Shhh, now listen.
I'll say it over.*

You were alone, I got you to sing.
You were quiet, I made you tell long stories.
No one knew who you were,
but they do now.

I have lived on the lip
of insanity, wanting to know reasons,
knocking on a door. It opens.
I've been knocking from the inside!

There's no love in me without your being,
no breath without that. I once thought

I could give up this longing, then thought again,
But I couldn't continue being human.

We are the night ocean filled
with glints of light. We are the space
between the fish and the moon,
while we sit here together.

Sometimes afraid of reunion, sometimes
of separation: You and I, so fond of the notion
of a *you* and an *I*, should live
as though we'd never heard those pronouns.

Two strong impulses: One,
to drink long and deep,
the other,
not to sober up too soon.

The wine we really drink is our own blood.
Our bodies ferment in these barrels.
We give everything for a glass of this.
We give our minds for a sip.

Wine to intensify love,
fire to consume, we bring these,
not like images from a dream reality,
but as an actual night to live through until dawn.

In complete control, pretending control,
with dignified authority, we are charlatans.
Or maybe just a goat's hair brush in a painter's hand.
We have no idea what we are.

We donate a cloak to the man who does the washing.
We feel proud of our generosity.
We stare at the infinite, suffering ocean.
We fall in.

You are cold, but you expect kindness.
What you do comes back in the same form.
God is compassionate, but if you plant barley,
don't expect to harvest wheat.

Wandering the high empty plain
for some indication you've been here,
I find an abandoned body,
a detached head.

Wine and stout,
one very old and the other new.
We will never have had enough.

Not being here and being completely here,
the mixture is not bitter.
It's the taste we are.

Lying back in this presence,
no longer able to eat or drink,
I float freely
like a corpse in the ocean.

Don't give me back to my old companions.
No friend but you. Inside you
I rest from wanting. Don't let me
be that selfishness again.

You reach out wanting the moon with your eyes,
and Venus. Build a place to live
with those dimensions. A shelter that can be
knocked down with one kick,
go ahead and knock it down.

Sometimes visible, sometimes not, sometimes
devout Christians, sometimes staunchly Jewish.
Until our inner love fits into everyone,
all we can do is take daily these different shapes.

My work is to carry this love
as comfort for those who long for you,
to go everywhere you've walked
and gaze at the pressed-down dirt.